# SAYINGS & DOINGS
## AND
# AN EASTWARD LOOK

# SAYINGS & DOINGS

## AND

# AN EASTWARD LOOK

WENDELL BERRY

GNOMON

LCCC NUMBER: 90-81977

ISBN 10: 0-917788-43-5

ISBN 13: 978-0-917788-43-7

This book contains the poems which first appeared in *An Eastward Look* published by Sand Dollar and *Sayings & Doings* published by Gnomon Press, with additions to both of those collections. The author would like to thank the following publications where some of these poems first appeared: *Monk's Pond, Green River Review, Lillabulero, Florida Quarterly, The Nation, Harper's, Handsel, Blue-Tail Fly* and *Place*. Sources for the 'Chinese Painting Poems' are *Art Treasures of the Peking Museum* (Harry N. Abrams) and *Chinese Painting* (Skira).

The publisher wishes to thank Christopher Meatyard for the use of his father's photograph for this book's cover. The art used for the part-title of *Sayings & Doings* is a detail of 'Tall Tales' by Wallace Kelly. The art used for the part-title of *An Eastward Look* was adapted by Laura Lee Cundiff from a detail of 'Reading in Autumn' by Shen Chou.

*Published by* Gnomon Press, P.O. Box 475,
Frankfort, KY 40602-0475

# CONTENTS

# SAYINGS & DOINGS

# I. REMEMBERING
# OLD TIMES

I used to know as many people
in Carroll County as I did
in Henry—or more. I used to go
to the Sanders Fair and spend
all day shaking hands and talking
to people I knew. And then
one time Jim took me to a sale
over there, and I saw nobody
I knew, and every one I asked about
was dead. I hung around,
talking a little here and there
asking about this one and that
one, and always getting the same
answer. Dead. Dead. Finally
I said, 'Jim, you see anything here
you want?' He said, 'No,'
and I said, 'Then let's go home.'

There used to be terrible times here.
Cheap tobacco. Bad markets. The crop
sometimes wouldn't pay what it cost
to sell it. After one hard time
when the market got better, an old man
I knew came up to me at the sale
and said, 'Well, Harry, we made it,
and we didn't commit suicide, did we?'
And I thought to myself, 'No,
but you've thought about it.'

The first time I remember waking up
in the night was in the winter time
when I was about six. Papa had sent
the tobacco crop to Louisville
to be sold, and we sat by the fire
that night, talking and wondering
what it would bring. It was a bad time.
A year of a man's work might be worth
nothing. And papa got up at two o'clock.
And I woke up and heard him leaving.
He saddled his horse and rode over
to the railroad, four miles, and took
the train to Louisville, and came back
in the dark that night, without a dime.

I remember when there weren't
but three newspaper subscriptions
in the whole town.
Mr. Mathews took one.
My father and his partner took one.
And Mr. Cunning took one.
When the mail came, the men
would gather in the stores
and read the paper,
and then they would argue.
Each one would stand up
and give his side, making
a regular speech, and then
somebody on the other side
would stand up and answer.
They usually left in a good humor.
Nobody ever changed his mind.

Lord, I've seen some *hard* fights
here. On election day
they'd come in out of the hollows
and fight as long as there was one
standing. Once I saw
a big red-headed fellow draw a circle
in the middle of the road,
and get in it, and dare
whoever came by to put him out.
Somebody finally did.

One day my father was coming
through town, and the air
was flying full of rocks
like a flock of birds passing over,
and he said, 'Boys,
if you all don't stop that
and go to shooting
somebody's liable to get hurt.'

## II. UNCLE RAD MILTON
## AND THE PUP

Uncle Rad wasn't what you'd call
an alcoholic, it was just
if there was any whiskey around
he'd drink it till either it
was gone or he was. Every time
his wife let him out of sight
he'd get on his old mare and go
to the saloon at town. He'd found
out how he could set a thing
in motion there that would go on
as long as he could stand it.
If he could get there early
and be the first one at the bar
he'd buy a drink for himself and one
for the next man to come in,
who would then buy a drink
for himself and Uncle Rad
and the *next* man, and so
it went, till he was hanging
on the bar by his elbows. All that

for just fifty cents. And then
they'd help him onto the old mare
and send him home again. Once,
one cold blowing winter day, Uncle Rad
slipped off to town, and hitched
the mare, and was first in the saloon.
He warmed himself until the fated
next man came in, obedient
to the providence that looked after
Uncle Rad. And Uncle Rad lubricated
and set in motion the benign machine
of his neighbors' generosity. It went
well that day as ever. The tilt
of his glass worked its old spell, and he
forgot the bad language
of any woman or any cold wind. The day
went on, until one came in
with a litter of hound pups in a box
to give away, and Uncle Rad claimed
his pup, and went back to the bar.
The clamor of the whiskey rose
in his head till he could no longer hear
the roar of the fire in the stove,
and then he had to spread his feet
to stand, and then he had to hang on
with his elbows. And then he said
he was going home, for he knew
when to quit. He rathered they'd say
'There he goes' than 'Here he lays.'

So they led him out and helped him
up on the old mare and headed her
the right direction—and one of them
said, 'What about his dog?' And they all
stood around then, and thought.
For there was a problem. The pup
was long-legged, a clumsy load,
and Uncle Rad needed one hand
to guide the mare and the other one
to hold on with, and he didn't have
a pocket big enough. They stood
around, shaking in the cold, squinting
hard through the mist of their breath,
thinking. And finally one of them
saw it through. 'Put it in his pants,'
he said. So they hauled Uncle Rad
down off the mare and opened his coat
and shoved the dog into his overalls
and set him on again. This time
he started home. He settled down
in a kind of grim drowse to endure
the cold wind and the long way,
till it hit him that he was bound
to pee. There was a problem, and he
shook himself and took thought.
He wasn't but halfway home,
and he couldn't wait. And though
he figured he could get down
well enough, he knew if he did

he'd never get back up again.
That wouldn't do. He tried to hurry.
He kicked the mare into a trot,
but every time her hoof struck
he throbbed like a dinner bell. 'Whoa!'
he said, and he took thought.
He would get relief, he declared,
from the mare's very back, though whether
such a feat had ever been performed
in history before, he didn't know.
He doubted it, in fact. But necessity
imposes wonders of its own,
and he tiptoed in the stirrups,
and leaned, propping his left hand
on top of the old mare's head—no easy
matter with the whole countryside
tilting and whirling past him as if
it was going on home, even if he
wasn't. And the old mare, thinking
of her stall, wasn't so still either
as she might have been. 'Stand still,
won't you, damn you! Whoa!' he said.
With his old fingers numb as sticks
he fumbled through the buttons
of three layers of clothes, and finally
caught hold and let go, aiming
at the ground over the mare's shoulder.
And he felt something running down
his leg, comfortably warm, but too wet

for cold weather. And he took thought.
'No,' he said, and let go again and felt
something warm running down his leg.
In such a circumstance, he thought,
a man should not trust appearances,
and this time he persevered to the end,
gazing at the sky in blessed relief.
And then it seemed to him that water
had steadily risen in his boot.
Was what he had done a dream?
He looked down then, and saw
in his hand the hind leg of the pup.

# III. SAYINGS & DOINGS

'Pap, health officer said
you got to get them damn
hogs out of the house.
It ain't healthy.'

'You tell that son of a bitch
I've raised a many
a hog in this house,
and ain't lost one yet.'

———

I lead a pretty good
old bachelor's life.
Plenty to eat.
Plenty to drink.
Fish and hunt
when I want to.
Don't care nothin
about money. Wouldn't
give a quarter fer it.

———

Well, I reckon it's going to snow.
I seen the little snowbirds a-flying.

Well, now, I reckon them little
snowbirds got to fly somewheres
even when it ain't going to snow.

———————

I thought he finally
had a woman he could keep
—knock-kneed, cross-eyed, fat. And then
along comes a blind man.

———————

Try a little of everything,
you'll hit on something.

———————

Put it in their reach,
not in their lap.

———————

He lacks just two weeks
being a good farmer.

———————

It would have been
very provident of Providence
if He had made
a certain *proficiency* necessary
for procreation.

———————

*(lettuce for the in-laws)*

'Ain't that enough?'

'More than enough,
but I'd be ashamed
to send so little.'

———————

*'Billy, why
in the name of God
would you tie up with a woman
as ugly as she is?'*

'You see this watch?
That's a dollar case
but it's got a
hundred dollars worth of works in it.'

———————

*My grandfather, as a young boy,*
*getting on the train at Turner's Station,*
*is stopped in the aisle of the coach*
*by an old man with a white beard,*
*a stranger to him:*

'You're Mawg Perry's boy.'

'Yes sir.'

'I sometimes miss the dam.
I never miss the sire.'

---------

*H.C., his old mare having just fallen in*
*the creek bed and broken her neck:*

She never done
*that* before.

---------

If you want people to love their country,
let them own a piece of it.

---------

He'd cut the finest shaving
you ever saw, afraid
he'd use up his stick
and have to get up to get another one.

—————————

Boys, here's a team
of matched horses,
so much alike
I don't know which one
looks most like the other.
They'll work single
or double, best
on either side.

—————————

Don't ever buy all
the groceries
your wife sends you for.
You might not
get back to town
for a week.

—————————

They've worn this country out
and sowed it in automobiles.

—————————

I built a bridge
and it washed out.
I built another one
and *it* washed out.
So I gave up
and bought a pair of boots.

_____

'You talk about a big city.
New Orleans is a big
city.
We started out driving
one morning at sunup
and drove all day
and when the sun went down
we was still
in New Orleans.'

'How fast was you driving?'

_____

*(Saturday morning)*

'Well, Uncle Bill,
  going to town to get drunk?'

'Yes, and O Lord
  how I dread it.'

_____

*Having diagnosed pregnancy in the case*
*of a young girl, unmarried, the doctor*
*steps out onto the porch,*
*followed by the distraught mother:*

'Oh doctor, do you suppose
a man could have got to that child?'

'Well, a good big boy
could a done it.'

———————

*(the secretiveness of ginseng)*

Something worth forty dollars a pound, he can't
afford to be *too* much in the open.

———————

Tell a lie and stick to it
long enough, and it'll *come* true.

———————

Had to give up grave digging.
Could still get them dug
all right, but got so old
could barely get out.

———————

*J.B., on his first appearance at church, is called*
*on to pray:*

Oh Lord,
bless me and my son Kirby.
                              Amen.

———————

I rode up to the house
and there was your mammy
sitting there on the stile
waiting for me—the prettiest
*formed* little thing!

———————

Anybody can be
sane in this world
is crazy as hell.

———————

'My feet are cold,' one says
and the legless man replies:
'So are mine.
So are mine.'

———————

'That old cow you sold me,
I can't get her to give
as much milk as you did.'

'Maybe you milk her
more often than I did.'

———————

Nawsir! You ain't a gonna get
no titty till you get
that chew of terbacker out of your mouth!

———————

'How old were you
when you were weaned?'

'I could stand up
and suck.'

———————

*The father appears in town after
the birth of his tenth child:*

'Well, was it a boy or a girl?'

'I dog if I heard 'em say.'

———————

*(the cross-eyed lady)*

She was standing in the middle
of the week, looking
both ways at Sunday.

———

*Two old acquaintances meet again by chance
after a long time, one having grown deaf:*

'It's Stanley Gibbs, ain't it?'

'NAW! IT'S GEORGE WASHINGTON'S
BIRTHDAY!'

———

'Do you know the difference
between satisfied and content?'

'I'm satisfied you're crazy as hell,
and I'm not content to be with you.'

———

Six months before
I married Alice I thought
I could just eat her up.
Six months afterwards
I wished to the Lord I had.

———————

'How much
tobacco you got?'

'Pret' near
a right smart,
but not hardly
so much,
either.'

———————

My wife invited me to leave, and I'm
on a high, wide and handsome,
getting it out of my system.
I like to talk to you, it sort of
zips me up.

I want you to meet my wife.
She's one of these intellectual types.
She'd tear your weather-boarding off.

———————

'You go to hell.'

'I don't go to your house
  when you ain't home.'

———————

'She went through
  a lot, before she died.'

'We've all got to go through
  enough to kill us.'

———————

'When I'm dead, Nick,
  I want you to bury me yonder
  in the corner of the lot.'

'Boss, you got to go farther
  away from here than that.'

———————

You'd have to go to school
before they'd let you in
at the insane asylum.

———————

The ceiling fell in
at my house last night.
If it hadn't hit me
in the back of the head
it would have hit
the old lady right in the face.

———————

Can't fool Him
can we?

———————

Well,
way I feel
is like this.

If we really
knew what was best
for us, the Lord
would have asked us
before He done it to us.

———————

I've got a few
little conveniences,
and I'll declare
I'm worn
to death with 'em!

———————

These two cats
was a fighting,
and the bottom cat
climbed on the top cat's back,
and the bottom cat
climbed on the top cat's back,
and the bottom cat
climbed on the top cat's back,
and finally they went up
clean out of sight.
The hair was a-falling
for three days.

———————

*(the locusts)*

What they're trying
to say is Phaaa-*roh*!
But so many of 'em
talking at once you can't
tell *what* they say.

———————

I always like
to cut my boards
good and short.

If you cut 'em
too short, you can
always splice 'em.

If you cut 'em
too long, ain't much
you can do about it.

———————

All I want
is a good single-line mule
and a long row!

———————

*(a man who never stopped talking)*

He might have been
a pretty smart fellow,
but whatever he knew
he learnt it from hisself.

———————

'I'm lost.'

'Well, turn on
the light.'

'If I knew
where the light
was, damn it,
I wouldn't be
lost.'

———————

'Now *she's* a nice person.'

'Yep—fibs
a little, I reckon.'

'How do you know?'

'There ain't
that much truth.'

———————

We have to eat
early at our house.
Ain't got enough to eat
to feed a *hungry* man.

———————

That's not the south wind.
That's the north wind
going home.

—————

'I'm dying. Will you
pray for me?'

'O lord, bless
my drunken husband.'

'*Don't* tell Him
I'm drunk,
damn it! Tell Him
I'm sick.'

—————

Do like the old Dutchman
that built his stone wall
as wide as he built it high,
so when it fell over it would
still be tall enough.

—————

'Anything exciting going on?'

'Well, I reckon not.
I ain't excited.'

---

The mosquitoes down there
can stand flat-footed
and frig a turkey.

---

'Le's go! Le's go!'

'Les Go's dead
and his wife's a widder.
If you be good
you might get her.'

---

They'll never do worth a damn
as long as they have two choices.

---

'I've heard of you leaving home,
and laying out drunk,
and I know you cuss a little.
How come you don't gamble?'

'No son of a bitch is going
to snap his fingers
and pick up *my* money.'

————————

'Talk about rich ground! Why,
that would grow maidenheads.'

'Nope. Too rooty and rocky.'

————————

*(political analysis)*

The grass roots are too
busy growing
grass.

————————

You can tell a chopper
by his chips.

————————

The older the goat,
the harder the horn.

───────────

'Well. You been getting any?'

'Nope. You been missin some?'

───────────

Something better,
something better,
everybody talking about
something better!
The important thing
is to feel good, and
enjoy what you got
if it ain't nothing
but a rail pen.

───────────

*The old man, speaking of funerals:*

Some of these days
I'm going to go
to one too many.

───────────

I feel better at home
than anywhere else,
and so I stay at home.

Long as I stay at home
I don't spend no money.

I never went anywhere
in my life that I
didn't buy something
I didn't need.

They tell you you're going to get
a wonderful bargain.
But if you don't need it,
it ain't no bargain.

———

Hey!
You read
that book
you wrote?

———

*(in the windstorm)*

More power,
Lord, you ain't
shook her
hardly any!

# AN EASTWARD LOOK

*For my mother*

# I. HAIKU

The evening after
the dog died, her tracks are still
fresh in the wet path.

———————

Bright frost adrift
in the morning air, light light
drifting in the air.

———————

What the clover says:
we can make it new. We can
make it new again.

———————

The wind too has its
destination, but in the
other direction.

———————

The freckled lilies
of the woods. They've come again.
And I have met them.

# II. A LONG JOURNEY &
# A SMALL NOTEBOOK

I.

Having made the place
neat, getting ready to go,
I wish I could stay.

2.

When I come again
winter will be past, the light
of spring on the river.

3.

The peach trees now dark
in leaves will be light in bloom
when I come back.

4.

During the absence
of the swallows I'll be gone,
the barn empty of flight.

5.

To be free a while
of the old duties! I pack,
thinking of mountains.

6.

Last year I thought it
important. Yesterday I
threw it in the fire.

7.

Farewell to the old.
A long journey and a small
notebook, a new form.

8.

In the sunset wind
one tree swaying on a hill,
two lovers dancing.

9.

Leaving the campground
before dawn, passing from sleep
to the road again.

10.

Our predecessors—
lost to their landmarks, gravemarks,
old boards, a few stones.

11.

Gone for good. The weeds
grow around the porch, windows
gaze through broken glass.

12.

Confess. You're afraid
the end of the world will come
before you make it home.

13.

Through hills, boulders, pines,
crooked simplification,
the rising footpath.

14.

Through the sage—a mile
a mile, a mile, a mile, O
wearying engine.

# III. CHINESE PAINTING POEMS

## The Sage's Hut in Autumn

Solitude, rain and wind, the night cold.
The tracks leading here have disappeared.
As I write, dipping my pen
in the flow, two white cranes
rise, and pass into the mist.

*After the painting and poem by Ni Tsan*

# The Storm Breaks

As he crosses the lake
in his small boat, suddenly
the trees, the reeds, the air
are leaning again him.

*After an unsigned painting*

# In Front of the Waterfall

The lives of the rock:
the water straight with falling,
the old tree twisted and bent
with hanging on.

*After the painting attributed to Ma Lin*

## Landscape with Snow

Cold and dim, the winter day
stands still over the snow
that clings to all but the river.
His boat drawn up to the porch,
the fisherman is selling his catch.
On the path there is one bent,
coming home with his load. Endless,
this business of keeping alive.

*After the painting by Li T'ang*

## Reading in the Autumn

The trees are already half bare.
I loosen my collar and let the time go.
At earth's verge I turn my back to the year,
doing nothing, nothing to do,
thoughts wandering in the air.

*After the painting and poem by Shen Chou*

# Landscape

Winding out of the hills,
the small stream enters the river.
It began coming down
long before these trees arrived.
In his boat the fisherman waits
like the hills along the stream
for what will be brought to him
and what will be taken away.

*After the painting by Wu Chen*

## A River Journey at First Snowfall

Lonely, lonely. The first snow
arrives, the wind driving it
among the dry blades of the reeds.
Travelers pass down the channel,
hurry on. Those who go
nowhere, but must sit cold, watching
their lines, imagine the day
closing, the travelers arriving
in a bright warm room.
The snowflakes melt in the river
quick as they touch, disappear.
It will be long until evening.
The winter will be long.

*After a section of a scroll by Chao Kan*

## Dreaming of Immortality
## in a Thatched Cottage

In this sad world where
if we're not hurting we're
itching, how good it is
that occasionally we should
escape, as now this one
has done. Asleep, his chin
resting on his folded arms,
he is no longer there
in the little house perched
on the mountainside. Free
of that stone hump pushing
up under its boulders
with all its weight, he is
standing in the air.

*After the painting by Chou Che'en*

# Watching the Mid-Autumn Moon

Young, we had not enough
respect for the changing moon.
Then the days seemed to pass
only to return again.
Now, having learned by loss
that men's days part from them
forever, we eat and drink
together beneath the full moon,
acknowledging and celebrating
the power that has bereft us
and yet sheds over the earth
a light that is beautiful.

*After the painting and poem by Shen Chou*

This book was set in Stempel Garamond
and printed on acid-free paper
by Thomson-Shore, Inc.